Better Homes and Gardens®

TRAINS & RAILROADS

Hi! My name is Max. I have some great projects to show you – and they're all about trains! We're going to have lots of fun making them together.

Inside You'll Find...

In the Train Yard

Max is in the train yard standing by Engine 51, a steam locomotive. Can you find him? Max likes to look at all of the things in the train yard. But wait! Max has found 10 items that don't belong in a train yard. Can you point to them?

4

Train Cars

A train has many kinds of cars. Each car has a different name. Look at the little pictures below and find the car that matches it in the big picture at the left.

Steam locomotive and coal tender

Hopper car

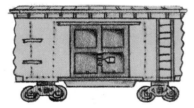

Boxcar

Tank car

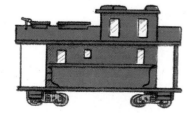

Caboose

5

Pufferbilly

Here comes a Pufferbilly, puffing down the railroad track. Puff, puff, chug, chug. Watch it go! You can make your own Pufferbilly using circles, squares, triangles, and rectangles.

What you'll need...

- One 9x12-inch sheet of construction paper
- Train Parts (see page 30)
- White crafts glue
- Scissors (optional)
- Crayons (optional)

1 Place the 9x12-inch sheet of construction paper on your working surface with a long side toward you (see photo).

To make the train cab, glue 1 of the rectangles from the Train Parts on the construction paper (see photo).

To make the engine, glue the other rectangle on the paper (see photo).

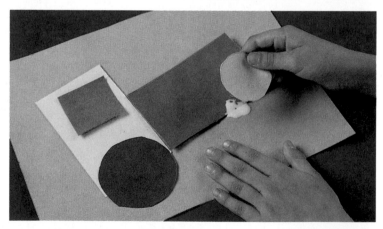

2 To make the window, glue the square on the top half of the train cab (see photo).

To make the rear wheel, glue the large circle at the bottom of the train cab (see photo).

To make the front wheel, glue the small circle at the bottom of the engine (see photo).

3 To make the smokestack, glue 1 of the triangles on top of the engine, toward the front (see photo). To make the cowcatcher, glue the other triangle at the front of the engine, toward the bottom (see photo).

If you like, cut around your Pufferbilly and use crayons to draw an engineer in the window (see photo on page 7).

Box Engine

Clickety-clack, down the track go many kinds of train cars. The most important car is the engine, because it pulls all the other cars. You can make an engine from empty shoe boxes, a cardboard tube, and a few other things.

What you'll need...

- 2 empty shoe boxes
- Crayon or pencil
- Scissors
- Tape
- One 4½-inch cardboard tube
- 4 jar lids or 4 poster board circles
- Extra-tacky white crafts glue
- One 4x4-inch piece of construction paper

1 To make the engine pieces, place 1 shoe box on end inside the other shoe box. With a crayon, on the inside shoe box trace along the edge where the 2 boxes meet (see photo).

Pull apart the 2 shoe boxes. Cut along the drawn line.

Decorate the cardboard tube any way you like.

2 To make the smokestack, tape the decorated tube to the end of the smaller piece of cut shoe box (see photo). Place the smokestack in the front end of the whole shoe box. To make the train cab, stand the larger piece of cut shoe box up in the back of the whole shoe box. To make the wheels, glue 2 jar lids on each side of the shoe box.

3 To make the cowcatcher for the front of the train, fold back about 1 inch along 1 side of the piece of construction paper.

Decorate the cowcatcher any way you like. Glue the folded edge to the front of the train (see photo). Decorate the engine any way you like.

Box Train Cars

Add to your train by making these train cars for your Box Engine to pull.
● Passenger car: use a shoe box without the lid.
● Tank car: use a round oatmeal box (18 ounces).
● Flat car: use the lid of a shoe box turned upside down.

A-l-l Aboard

The train is about to leave and the conductor shouts, "All aboard!" Max and Marci need to hurry and load their luggage. Can you count how many suitcases they have?

Matching Luggage

Can you find the 4 suitcases in the picture on the left that match the 4 suitcases below? Be careful. There may be some that are almost the same, but not quite right.

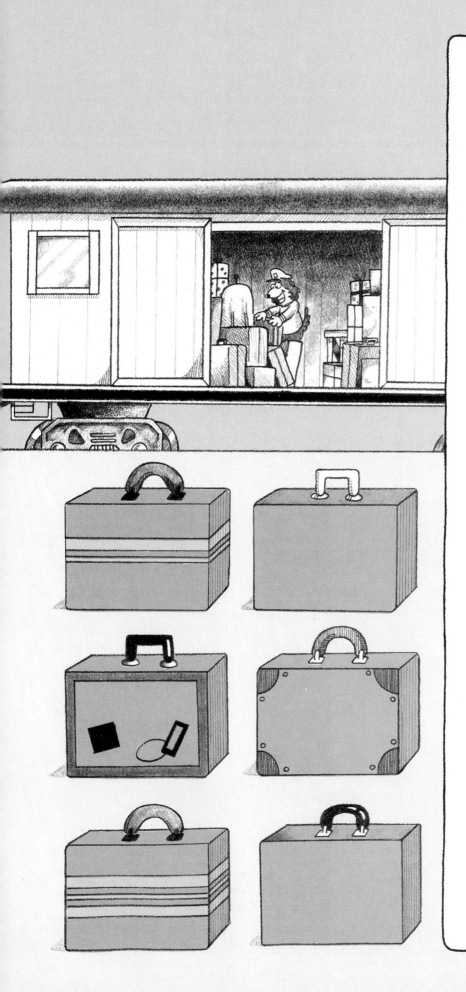

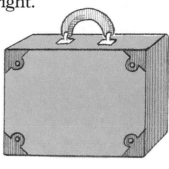

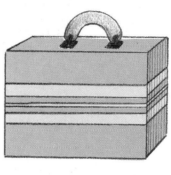

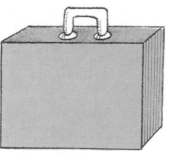

Conductor's Hat

A conductor is the person who makes sure the passengers get on the train safely and get to where they want to go. What would you do if you were a conductor? All conductors wear hats, and so can you.

What you'll need...

- Scissors
- 1 paper plate
- Crayons, markers, or colored pencils
- One 3x24-inch piece of construction paper
- Tape or white crafts glue

1 To make the hat's brim, cut the paper plate in half.
Starting at the middle of the straight edge, cut toward the outside of the plate, stopping about 2 inches from the edge. Make 2 more cuts in the plate for a total of 3 cuts (see photo).

2 Place the paper plate upside down with the straight edge away from you.
Fold the cut portions up to form triangles (see photo).
Decorate the curved brim any way you like.

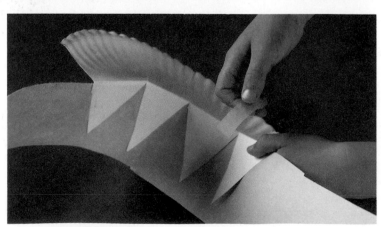

3 For the hat's band, decorate the piece of construction paper any way you like.
Place the band behind the brim's points. Secure the band to the points with tape (see photo).
With adult help, fit the band around your head so it is comfortable. Tape the band closed at this point.

Railroad Tickets

When going for a ride on the train, you need a ticket.

To make your own ticket, decorate a 3x5-inch piece of construction paper or a 3x5-inch index card. If you like, cut a half circle from each end to make it look more like a real ticket.

Traveling Suitcase

Going on a trip? What are you going to take along? Max always likes to put his toothbrush, pajamas, coloring books, and crayons in a suitcase. This easy-to-make suitcase can hold lots of your favorite things.

What you'll need...

- Suitcase Labels (see tip on page 15)
- One 6x9-inch piece of construction paper
- 1 empty pop can box (12 pack)
- Tape
- Pencil
- Yarn, cotton twine, or string, about 20 inches long

1 Use Suitcase Labels to decorate the construction paper and the pop can box any way you like.

To make the side pocket, tape 1 end of the construction paper to 1 side of the box. Then tape the opposite end of the paper to the box. Finish by taping the bottom edge of the paper to the box (see photo).

2 To make suitcase handle, use the pencil to punch 2 holes about 6 inches apart on 1 side of the box. Thread the yarn down through 1 hole and back up through the other (see photo). Bring the ends together. Tie a knot.

To make threading easier, wrap the ends of the yarn with a small piece of tape.

Suitcase Labels

Decorate your suitcase with these fun labels.

- Use coloring book pictures.
- Cut out pictures from magazines.
- Use bumper stickers.
- Create your own labels with construction paper and crayons.

Signs and Signals

Hey look! Max sees the Railroad Crossing sign. He knows to stop and wait. Besides the letters in the sign, the letters T, R, A, I, and N are hidden in the picture below. Can you find the letters?

Train Signals

Do you know what these train signs and signals are called?

1 Railroad Crossing Ahead

2 Railroad Crossing

3 Railroad Crossing— lights flash and the arm comes down when a train crosses the road

1

2

3

Painted RR Signs

You'll be right on track to a delicious snack when you make these delightful cookies. Max always likes a cold glass of milk with his cookies.

What you'll need...

- 1 table knife
- One 20-ounce roll refrigerated sugar cookie dough
- 2 cookie sheets
- 30 wooden sticks
- 1 table fork
- 1 egg yolk
- ¼ teaspoon water
- 2 small bowls
- Red and green food coloring
- 2 *new* paintbrushes, washed
- Wire cooling rack

1 With adult help, preheat the oven to 350°.

Using the knife, cut a ¼-inch-thick slice from the roll of cookie dough (see photo). Place a wooden stick on an ungreased cookie sheet, about 3 inches from the side. Place dough slice atop stick. Repeat with remaining sticks and dough, placing sticks 3 inches apart.

2 Pat out each slice of dough with your fingers to about 3 inches in diameter (see photo).

In a small mixing bowl use a fork to mix together the egg yolk and water. Pour some of the yolk mixture into each of the 2 small bowls. Add about 3 drops of food coloring to each bowl. Stir together.

3 With the egg yolk mixture, paint a big X on the dough. Then paint the letter R on each side of the X (see photo).

With adult help, bake in a 350° oven for 7 to 11 minutes or till golden. Remove cookie sheets from the oven. Let cookies cool for 1 minute. Remove and cool on a wire rack. Makes about 30.

Toot-Toot Whistle

TOOT, TOOT. . . . Max can hear the train as it comes down the railroad tracks. Do you know what the train is saying? See the tip on page 21 to find out what the different signals mean.

What you'll need...

- Crayons, markers, or colored pencils
- One 3¼x10-inch piece of construction paper
- 1 empty plastic pop bottle, rinsed and drained
- Tape
- String or yarn, about 24 inches long

1 Use the crayons to decorate the paper on 1 side any way you like.

Lay the pop bottle on the undecorated side of the paper. Wrap the paper around the bottle. Tape the paper in place (see photo).

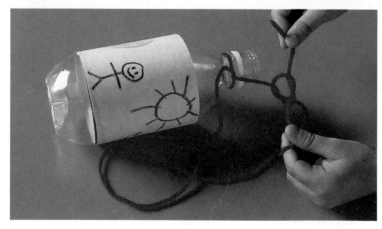

2 Tie the string around the neck of the bottle.

Adjust the length of the string so the bottle can hang around your neck. Tie the ends together in a knot (see photo).

To make your whistle TOOT, TOOT like a real train whistle, blow across the top of the bottle.

Train Signals

Try these signals for talking with your train.
- 1 long blast - The train is coming into the station.
- 1 short blast - Stop!
- 2 short blasts - Watch out! The train is starting to move.
- Short repeated blasts - Get off the tracks!

Railroad Lantern

People who work on trains use lanterns to tell the engineer driving the train when to stop and when to go. You can make your lantern in your favorite color. Look on page 32 for signals you can use when playing with your lantern.

What you'll need...

- Newspaper or brown kraft paper (optional)
- Tempera paint
- Paintbrushes
- One 1-quart milk or juice carton, rinsed
- Scissors
- Foil
- Pencil
- 1 pipe cleaner or 12-inch string

1 If desired, cover your work surface with newspaper.

To make a lantern, paint the empty milk carton. Let it dry.

Cut 4 shapes any way you like from the foil. Glue 1 foil shape, shiny side up, on 1 side of the milk carton (see photo). Repeat with remaining foil shapes.

2 Decorate the lantern around the foil shapes any way you like (see photo).

3 With adult help, use a pencil to punch 2 holes on the top of the milk carton.

To make the handle, put a pipe cleaner through the holes (see photo). Then twist the ends together.

Traveling by Train

Max and Marci enjoy an ice-cream sundae in the dining car. The waiter is serving them water, but something's wrong. There are 10 things missing from inside the dining car. Can you name them?

Tube-Body Travelers

Have you ever been a passenger on a train? You can do many of the same things on the train that you do at home — sit, talk, sleep, read, eat, and walk. These travelers can be passengers on your Box Engine and Box Train cars.

What you'll need...

- Crayons or pencils
- One 4½-inch cardboard tube
- 2 muffin papers
- Scissors
- Tape
- Yarn or ribbon
- Pencil

1 Using a crayon, draw a face on the tube. Decorate the body any way you like.

To make the skirt, use a muffin paper. With the scissors, cut into the center of the muffin paper and cut the bottom out (see photo).

Wrap the paper around the tube. Secure with tape.

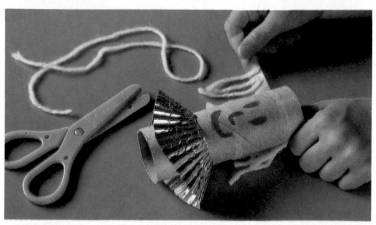

2 To make the yarn hair, place several strips of yarn side by side so they are touching.

Cut a piece of tape that is longer than the width of all the yarn pieces. Lay the tape across the top of the yarn strips.

Stick the tape with the yarn around the back of the tube near the top edge (see photo).

3 To make the hat, put glue on the inside of the remaining muffin cup. Place the top of the tube in the muffin cup (see photo). Let glue dry.

What other kinds of people do you think will be traveling on the train?

Fancy Hats

To make various hats, use jar lids, nut cups, or create your own. To make a cone hat, cut a 4-inch circle out of paper. Then cut a pie-shaped wedge out of the circle (cut out about ¼ of the circle). Bring the cut ends together and overlap them slightly to make a cone shape. Tape the ends together.

Dining Car Sundae

When Max rides on a passenger train, he eats in a special train car called the dining car. It's like a restaurant on wheels. For dessert, Max always likes to order an ice cream sundae. Now you can create your own sundae!

What you'll need...

- 3 small spoons
- Choo-Choo Chocolate Sauce (recipe on page 32) or chocolate-flavored syrup
- 1 dessert dish
- 1 ice cream scoop or large spoon
- Vanilla ice cream
- Fresh fruit
- Granola
- Semisweet chocolate pieces

1 To make your sundae, use a spoon to put some Choo-Choo Chocolate Sauce in the bottom of your dish. Use the ice cream scoop to place ice cream on the sauce.

2 Using another small spoon, place some fresh fruit on top of the ice cream.

3 Then with the first spoon, top your fruit with more Choo-Choo Chocolate Sauce.

Make a Sundae Any Day

To build a super-delicious sundae, pick and choose the sauce, ice cream, fruit, and topping you like best. What's your favorite combination?

Sauces
- Choo-Choo Chocolate Sauce (see page 32)
- Tootie Fruity Sauce (see page 32)
- Marshmallow creme
- Caramel ice-cream sauce
- Honey

Ice Cream
- Vanilla
- Strawberry
- Chocolate
- Butter Pecan

Fruits
- Nectarine slices or canned peach slices, drained
- Bananas, sliced
- Fresh straw-berries, sliced, or frozen unsweetened whole strawberries, thawed
- Fresh pineapple chunks or canned pineapple tidbits, drained

Toppings
- Granola
- Chopped peanuts or sunflower nuts
- Toasted coconut
- Animal crackers
- Semisweet chocolate pieces
- Maraschino cherries

4 Finish off your sundae with granola and chocolate pieces. Eat and enjoy right away!

In the Train Yard

See pages 4 and 5

As your children complete this activity, explain that trains go to a train yard at the end of a trip. The locomotives and other cars are cleaned and repaired in the train yard. Then, they are ready to begin another journey.

The train in the picture on pages 4 and 5 is a freight train. Freight trains can carry food, furniture, animals, toys, and other things all across the country.

In addition to the train cars shown in the picture, a freight train may include:

Refrigerator car: carries fruits, vegetables, flowers, and other items that must be kept cold.

Gondola car: a car without a roof. It carries steel, concrete blocks, and other items that won't be damaged by rain or snow.

Autoveyer: a triple-deck car that carries automobiles.

Flat car: a platform carrying tractors, logs, or trailer trucks.
● Reading suggestions:
Freight Train
  by Donald Crews
The Little Engine That Could
  by Watty Piper

Pufferbilly

See pages 6 and 7

Before your children start the project, you will need to cut out the Train Parts from construction paper. Our kid testers told us they liked to use as many different colors of construction paper as possible. For each Pufferbilly, you will need:

two 3x5-inch rectangles
one 2-inch square
one 1½-inch square, cut
  diagonally (2 triangles)
one 3-inch circle
one 2-inch circle

Your children can create many other designs with these shapes. Provide plenty of cut-outs in different shapes, sizes and colors. To help your children get started, suggest they make a car or boat from the different shapes.

Box Engine

See pages 8 and 9

Once your children have completed the Box Engine and 1 or more Box Cars, they can make a Box Train and a Train Set. Here's how:

Box Train: Punch a hole with a paper punch or pencil in the back of the engine and in the front of a car. Thread a piece of string or yarn through the hole in the engine. Tape the end of the string to the inside. Thread the other end of string through the hole in the car and tape in place. Make your train as long as you like.

Your children may wonder how the steam engine earned the funny nickname pufferbilly. A steam engine in England once was nicknamed "puffing billy." Billy is a British word similar to the American term buddy. Over the years the name was shortened to pufferbilly and was applied to any steam engine.

Train Set: Make buildings, mountains, and trees for the train set. Draw a train station, school, house, or mountains on a piece of poster board or white cardboard. Cut out your drawing, leaving about 1 inch of poster board below the drawing. To make your scenery stand, fold back the 1 inch of poster board below the drawing.

For stand-up trees, draw 2 identical trees on a piece of poster board, cardboard, or construction paper. Cut a slit in 1 of the trees, from the top to the middle. Cut a slit in the other tree, from the bottom to the middle. Slide the trees together. To make the tree stand, be sure the pieces meet at right angles (see photo).

A-L-L Aboard

See pages 10 and 11

Young children enjoy imaginary play, and especially like having their parents join in the play-acting.

Ask your children where they would like to go on a train trip. You may be surprised by the faraway places their imaginations will take them. When we invited children to test the train projects for this book, they pretended they were taking train trips to Florida, Africa, and an amusement park.

Ask your children questions such as:

What would you pack in your suitcase? What would you do for fun? How long would you stay?

● Reading suggestions:
The Polar Express
　by Chris Van Allsburg
The Train to Grandma's
　by Ivan Gantschev

Conductor's Hat

See pages 12 and 13

With different decorations, this hat turns into a birthday party hat. You and your children can make hats for each guest. Decorate the hats with glitter, stickers, and press-on bows.

Or, make a top hat for President Lincoln's birthday or a Pilgrim's hat for Thanksgiving. Use black construction paper and color or paint the paper plate black.

Traveling Suitcase

See pages 14 and 15

Here's another suitcase your children can make:

Place 1 sheet of construction paper on top of another sheet. Staple the sheets together along 1 long side and both of the short sides. Leave 1 long side open. If you like, draw lines along the stapled sides to resemble stitching.

Cut 2 handles from another sheet of construction paper. Staple or tape 1 handle to each sheet of construction paper on the open side. Now the suitcase is ready to hold your children's drawings and letters.

Sign and Signals

See pages 16 and 17

The picture illustrates how important it is to obey traffic signs. Take this opportunity to remind your children to always stop for a flashing rail-

road crossing sign or when the signal arm is down. Also, explain that they should never play near railroad tracks.

Review with them street safety rules, such as asking permission to cross a street and looking both ways before crossing it.

Painted RR Signs

See pages 18 and 19

Here are some other railroad signs that your children can use with the Box Engine and Box Train on pages 8 and 9.

For the post, press a craft stick or pipe cleaner into a cork or an egg carton cup. Use craft sticks or construction paper cutouts to make the sign. Draw lights with crayons or markers. Glue or tape the sign to the post.

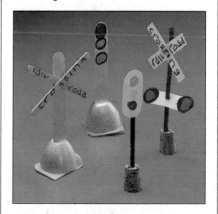

Toot-Toot Whistle

See pages 20 and 21

Our kid testers loved this project. When asked why, they told us they liked the funny sounds the whistle made. One child pretended the pop bottle was a musical instrument and another child pretended it was a car horn.

You may need to show your children how to blow over the top of the bottle to make it whistle. Of course, children will need to blow harder than you do because of their smaller

size. Be patient and eventually they will figure out how to blow to make the loudest sound.
● Reading suggestion: *Little Toot* by Hardie Gramatky

Railroad Lantern

See pages 22 and 23

Before the days of electric signals, lanterns were used to signal engineers at night. During the day, a black ball on a rope was used. Whether they used the lantern or the ball, the signals were the same.
Stop: swing the lantern back and forth in front of the knees.
Go: raise and lower the lantern from shoulders to knees.

Traveling by Train

See pages 24 and 25

The train shown on these pages is a passenger train. Even though a passenger train includes an engine and caboose, its other cars differ from those found on a freight train.
Coach: contains rows of upholstered seats that recline.
Dining car: contains both the kitchen and the dining room. This is where the passengers eat meals.
Sleeping car: contains beds for overnight trips.
Baggage car: holds your suitcases and other luggage.
Dome car: has a glass ceiling. Passengers can ride in this car and look at the mountains, trees, and other scenery.

Tube-Body Travelers

See pages 26 and 27

The Tube-Body Travelers can travel in the Box Engine or Box Car (see pages 8 and 9). Besides Tube-Body Travelers of all types, children can make a Tube-Body Engineer to drive the Box Engine and a Tube-Body Conductor to take the tickets from the Tube-Body Travelers.

Dining-Car Sundaes

See pages 28 and 29

Both of these sauces make delicious ice cream toppings.

Choo-Choo Chocolate Sauce

    1½ cups tiny marshmallows
    ¾ cup milk
    1 6-ounce package (1 cup) semisweet chocolate pieces

● In small saucepan combine marshmallows and milk. Cook and stir over medium heat till marshmallows are melted.
● Add chocolate pieces. Continue heating and stirring with a wire whisk till chocolate is melted. Remove from heat and cool slightly.
● Pour mixture into a serving dish. Cover and chill. Before serving bring to room temperature. Makes 2 cups.

Tootie Fruity Sauce

    ½ teaspoon finely shredded orange peel
    ¼ cup orange juice
    1 tablespoon cornstarch
    ¼ teaspoon ground cinnamon
    1 10-ounce package frozen strawberries, thawed

● In a medium saucepan mix orange peel, orange juice, cornstarch, and cinnamon. Stir in thawed strawberries.
● Cook and stir over medium heat till the mixture thickens and is bubbly. Cook and stir for 2 minutes more. Remove from the heat. Cool to room temperature.
● If you have any leftovers, put them in a covered container and chill. Makes 1⅓ cups.

BETTER HOMES AND GARDENS® BOOKS
Art Director: Ernest Shelton   Managing Editor: David Kirchner
Department Head, Food and Family Life: Sharyl Heiken

TRAINS AND RAILROADS
Editors: Sandra Granseth, Heidi McNutt, and Mary Major Williams
Graphic Designers: Harjis Priekulis and Linda Vermie
Project Manager: Jennifer Speer Ramundt
Contributing Photographer: Scott Little   Contributing Illustrator: Buck Jones

Have BETTER HOMES AND GARDENS® magazine delivered to your door.
For information, write to: ROBERT AUSTIN P.O. BOX 4536 DES MOINES, IA 50336